cloudfang

◆ ◆

◆ ◆

cakedirt

cloudfang :: cakedirt

Daniela Olszewska

HORSE LESS PRESS

First edition printed in the United States.

ISBN: 978-0-9829896-3-0

Cover art: "A Midnight Frolic" © 1897 by The H.C. Miner Litho. Co., N.Y. Courtesy of the Library of Congress Prints and Photographs Division in Washington, D.C.

Design & typesetting by HR Hegnauer | hrhegnauer.com

Typeset in Goudy Old Syle

The publication of this book was made possible through the generous contributions of our readers and supporters; we extend particular gratitude to Andy Brown, Maryrose Larkin and Eric Matchett, and Labmom53.

HORSE LESS PRESS

www.horselesspress.com

cloudfang

frontier w/ fancy spurs

you seep through the belly
of the stagecoach—definitely

w/o child or petticoat.
o, what a nice spot

for a ruckus or some goldfinch.
this is after the noon

starts becoming blazingly
territorial + you're providing

us w/ evidence of bad holler
+ tumbleweed sparkle.

everyone seems determined
to rarify yr constitutionals.

though, i am convinced
that the rest of our cowgirls

already hurt too much
from the hip up.

we could take to shooting
tin-rimmed buffalo

+ not hardly giving a damn,
            so don't stress, it's already well-

            known that some of our best
            friends also started out as ill-

            conceived + overly fond
            of the tenderhold.

[ ] [ ], [ ] [ ]

since moving here, i've daunted
+ dandelioned—amply comfortable

in my thwarted status. zoned
for inverted temperatures,

staying this inconsequential
is easier than pleasing w/ hooks.

the acres on the side accommodate
w/ melodic roots. there are hums

+ drums happening all along
the inside of strongthrob ears.

i thought i would be tonedeaf
or lonely, but most late afternoons

are so symphony, it's knifed thru
any missing that might be trying

to grow unrequited on or in
or anywhere near my open palm.

these curtains are hideous, but they go w/ everything

let us always
keep an affinity
for parlorsong

whilst wearing
bracelets made
of black pot

+ blacker kettle
parts stolen special
like a velvet tufted

doorprize during
that year everything
happened in hemispheres—

like the bottling up
of twelve involuntary
cloud complexes—

we steady ourselves
by announcing that,
actually, we are all

already out
of spare feelings—

but, indirectly, we laden
w/ hooks, we partner

down w/ a decent spot
of scotch whilst

the chambermusic,
the chambermusic, gets
noticeably more abrupt.

artifice rex

i plop triangle candy
in the saucers spaced
about the teahouse

while you called me
back until we were
both out of retina.

trifocaled + het-for-pay,
some paths turn out
quicker than others. must

guess: falsetto isn't much
to be bashful of.
otherwise, haters

are always getting
ready to _ _ _ _. see
also: swarm of porcelain flies.

see also: rows upon rows
of open caskets
rubbed in vim or vinegar.

garden partying for dummies

some skip amok.
w/ razors in
their figleaves,
they try + repent prettily.
                    but [the theoretical 'i'] never
was very keen on tattling
[on my theoretical 'self'].

[the theoretical 'i'] falls out of a tree
[the theoretical 'i'] covered in serpentskin.
[the theoretical 'i'] falls out of a tree
                          + into a puddle of melted tones.
          —under different circumstances,
          this could've been the perfect place
          to erect a gazebo—

a thing mingles inside [the theoretical 'me'].
the sky gets big + blemished
+ everywhere, everywhere

[the theoretical 'i'] + i keep gasping after
                          our secondtolast breath twice.

amateur gumshoe hour

hazard a pearl-
filled clue saturated

in tawdry noirlight.

    this is a corpsefloat—
    sprinkle gardenia

    trifles over black

velvet. an aversion
to pigeonsick

isn't that suspicious

under the goblinhard
moon—

    so go ahead + crack
jokes like knuckles 'n skulls—

the situation's already
truly arduous w/ mysterious scar

+ a ring of arson might end up solving
these several problems at once.

we like it when you call us *ladies of leisure*

on the way
to the blitz

they usually throw
after i've turned

my passport
towards etude,

you reveled
in yr sense

of bird's eye
whilst i felt myself

crashing
through a gate

all pearled
by proxy.

things to do in personform
(when something is better than nothing)

to swell in appleblossom. :::: to doubledare in stereo.

to east you by the holidayshore. :::: to oppositesex problem.

to refold the atlas proper. :::: to exculpate in capricorn.

to downslope on the mooncurved hill. :::: to unsheltered zoological.

to jazztap w/ magictophat. :::: to get up + at 'em on the plushside.

to bruise coyotecolored. :::: to alms. toalms.

to armcross w/o treasuretrove. :::: to wickerburn indefinite.

to sprinkle turquoisedrops. :::: to demeanorgood. to surfeitwell.

saint festive's illegitimate child

the top of this pinetree
is so electricfence.

i put an angelbow on it.
it was aflame. no one

appreciated the ornament
of my boyteeth rubbed

in brine. so, here is a polar-

                                        shark egg; hang it

from a lowbranch.
next solstice eclipse,

i want you to expect
better from me,

to insist i airtight,
like i can't carry a tune

in between these plush

pouches embroidered
                                        w/ silverthings.

after the phone tree died

i built an entire arboretum
around this single branch

of juniper. the berries
will come later or, probably,

not at all. there's the mark
of the pegasus clause

that makes me impossible
to act pretty. rest assured,

when dealing w/ mythological
content, it's best to learn

to properly disable the safety lock.
these diasters better just be a phase.

because i've a rather ill-informed
opinion of our abilities to prevent

forest fires in the midst of these droughts
going 40-nights strong in places
citizened by the hard-of-hearing.

now, in the prettiest part of the country

wearing a nest
of amber twigs,

shimmying up
+/or down a speckled

pole, need covering
in oatmeal + crushed

worm—there must be
a less humiliating way

to get another person
to care for +/or about you—

most of this should
mend back fine—though—

still tremble somewhat
in turmoil whenever

you feel a bout of green
+/or wings
w/ fringe coming on.

visitors' weekend

she comes via
briar patch

with a few
pulsing cow

hearts + low
utility belts.

we grope
for the accurate

pronunciation
of maybe.

like cannibal,
she snips

our red indoor
chemistries until

the postmortems
are performed

on a diagonal.
come sunday,

she puts a left
foot in + a right

arm out until
it's making a never

before seen dance
full of halfsteps
+ cloudfang.

how to cure yr own clubfoot

gauge the alarms,
all this post-stairwell

chaperoning is liable
to muck up yr sobriety

again. i will buy you
a sterling silver

skeleton w/ very fine
acoustics, spectacularized

in abacus beads + bird-
                    cage bottoms

if you promise
to slip it on under

that hairy skein
of skin you've got

tucked up there
in yr french + thriving
                    peony box.

squid +/or you

squid will never learn to tell the difference between a dolphin + a porpoise.
if there even is a difference. at sideshow practice, they tell you that it doesn't

actually matter. as long as you both annunciate cleanly + get the right
kind of tassels. as long as you are good at contortion sets.
tri-hearted + slow-thawed, squid knows

how to coax the titillate out of you. together, you practically double the
number of ducats the company earns during the coldblooding seasons.

squid takes to leaving deadlarks on yr doorstep. you share a tendency to
black out in 24-hour laundromats. he likes that you don't want to
sleep w/ him. or, he likes

that you don't want him to want to sleep w/ you. the first thing squid ever says
to you is that he has trouble learning names so can he please just call you squid.

also, he tells you that you should really start fleshing out yr mermaid's
muscle memory.

during one noon exhibition, squid + you crush somebody else's baby by
accident. squid wraps it in mesh + calls for a rimshot. you grossly
underestimate how long

it takes to calm down a hysterical mother when you're 2 leagues under.

so the mercury level rises + yr tap routine goes from bad to worse. people stop
pretending to be interested in squid's explanations for the tiny globes

inside the jellyfish. in tulsa, squid half-nelsons an autistic member of the
audience + screams that he will never know what it means to say

you don't kiss on the lips + management puts you on notice.

this feels like practically since forever ago. you guess that, by now
there is no sense in gearing up for the jubilee year.

still, you try + teach yrself to read sheet music. squid hints at an
upcoming geological event, at a plan for developing insomnia in
order to make the most

of the time left. this is about wanting to use yr powers for good, you
agree. about tying yr hands to squid's tentacles w/ lyre string +
insisting you both smile big about it.

@the dancehall

you know i try
out w/ the astrals

mentioned in passing.
my top

half went daisy
cutter weeks ago—

it was rather
spectacular—

the spread eagling
ballerina cultivated

a weak spot
on my wrist

while yr segues,
they petaled

in violent pastels.

in the armored clown car

w/ fossils on our breaths,
we floozy in tiny sequined hats.

you grease paint over
the only part of yr face

that doesn't actually need covering.

let's see, i found these keys
under the kitchen sink along

w/ those morbid curiosities
in ragtime. tulip-torn, we reconcile

my tastes w/ yrs. our personal
sadness is so great, it is skyscraper-

sized + holding a bloody
fucking seraph between its teeth.

but here is a mini parade
of camels clomp-clomping

across our laps + you are still
honking the horn like our favorite

team just trophied in the world
+ universal championships.

actually, neither of us deserves this certificate of completion

i am an emotion-
manufacturing machine,

even if the weather
won't get inclement

for you yet. corset-
tight in embellished cow

bodice + the awards hall
is filled w/ secret agents

hiding behind potted plastic
ferns—they are just twitching

to catch me pocketing
silverware from yr busy

date's place-setting. i wouldn't
care, though, if they took me out

in jerkhold + slack in the jaw.
i am *so soaked* in elderflower-

infused gin + who are *you*
to judge when you can't even

wear the right color tie
to a black tie event?

the eighth sea, the ninth wonder of the world

edged in salt or brine,
woebegone w/ fishnet,
i oracled at the end

of the mainline. you sipped
quinine + rolled turkish
fireflies under my thumb

whilst the rest of the ship
shaped sonars, we strove
to move about the sickles

again. this part-nocturne
ceaselessly stuns me
back into a sea-sorry state

of needing, of wanting for it
to be ≥ than whatever you had
already got to figuring on

vintage-ish, we fan ourselves

after our promenade past the barricade, we fold up parasols + start to talk
of matching mother-daughter cutlery.   fondly, we eye the curio
shelf in the corner.   it certainly contains a vial of polish.   you
remember yr poor consumptive antiques dealer, how she had to glue
the lace to the coffin edge herself.   we are so very fond of
france   + other european countries.   we are also so very fond of
chocolate-covered strawberries.   the woman who owns the natural
history museum tells us how to put pocket mirrors in   the mouths
of stuffed moose.   for the sake of the children, she says.   you
sing soprano over the roar of cloud-seeding guns.   someone makes his
or her disapproval heavy with good manners.   the footman twitches.
i gesture the company's attention in a direction. it is the direction of
the two oriental rugs.   between the two of them, you count five
hundred fuchsia spirals + six hundred turquoise star tips.   the bay
window casts people-ish shadows on the smaller rug.   a clock tocks.
we eat some strawberry-covered chocolates.   the drill sergeant's sister
claims to be hard at work   on a new card trick.   you think that
now we have such an excellent excuse for leaving early after coming late.

(the south is only a home)

her semi-successful recipe for swampthings

she made them
ground-dumb

w/ leg-lag
+ scratch patch.

some resistance
is circumstantial.

the mormon
wanted photographs.

they were smelling
of damp

roseheaded foster
child. she suspected

they would take
to quarreling

w/ weathervanes
+/or eating out

of the lawnmower
magnate's koi pond.

she figured that the centers
would eventually go mush.

o, her kitchen,
it smoldered, like

in the midst of losing
a very important
kind of argument.

designated driver

you aren't afraid of dying;
just afraid of being
permanently disfigured.
you are trying out
all four versions
of yr frosted
vegetable voice,
but the passengers
keep demanding
an explanation
of the difference
between a firecracker
+ a firework. try for
a rather ruthless joke,
then check to make
sure the check engine
light is still blinking
orange + not red.
the car goes over
a lot of already split
open opossums
+ a few tiny deer.
when the speed
limit ups to 65,
you start remembering
about elvis
+ the way the gas
station attendant
kept asking
if the hetero half
of yr heart
had even a little
bit of tennessee
left in it.

hearsay in mobile, alabama

there used to be
a phone basket

on every corner
+ a spigot in

the shrubbery
+ over there

a sailor halving
avocados while

his friend put
a plastic bag

over or under
their heads

while some snail-
scaled boats

lit up w/ finicky
blue dots.

in small southern towns, every autumn has at least one friday the thirteenth

fitted in wearing out madras +
seersucker, lob off
the whiteskin
of a summer
meat's wishbone,
it's obvious you've been rolling
about yr cousin's sugarbeets
w/ the aphids again.
as the town's team starts
looking not all that
stadium-ready, most
of your neighbors take to knocking
over your ladyladder + dyeing
rabbit's feet unrabbit-like colors.
meanwhile, the head
coach + you are memorizing
bus schedules while holding
pinkie swears under the pews
or outside the opposing
team's locker room.

on the correlation between thumb-sucking + promiscuity

audibly, visibly,
cradle the right
kind of stranger
danger   + jump
off the train bound
for mississippi.

            w/ surprisingly little
to hide, push
on the pheromone
monitor until
those magnolias fall
back into peripheral.

            the stranger helps
suture sweet yr fat finger
like it's that space
between love +
attention,
            though, o, it's terrible
            having to work
                        out the difference
w/ a thumb-map print of yr very own.

@the baggage claim

atlanta: left a full jar
of spiderlegs

in a plaid
suitcase checked

under a flower-
derivative kind

of nickname.

a lady who looked
like a nurse

+ talked a lot
about roller derby

waited for me
near the conveyor belt

w/ her hair curled + unclasped

                    the universe's
underdeveloped sense

of funnybone
was getting up to

it again.   though, this time,

i was determined to work hard
                    at playing
                    like i knew how
                    to stay cool.

you look sensational, you look barely related to me

we used, i think
to share a pawnshop-
owning uncle w/ a pacemaker
+ a brain
wet w/ rural
afterhours. a barnraising
tempo nudged
through the late
part of our chronic october.
disoriented, i restocked
the terrain w/ less
toxic squirrels
while you salvaged
the hubcaps
from the caddy
colored like
the insides
of a veterans' association.
o boy, lately, i barely
recognize you in
that outfit.
lately, we are both
30% bodyfat bag.
i worry that we are
unintentionally sharing
a toothbrush; i worry
that there is this ongoing
war against running
in circles + you might
quite possibly already
be up for the draft.

after yr last abortion, things got a little crazy

i put a firstplace
tangerine in yr wet

t-shirt pocket + we both
received more

than a few credibly
detailed death threats.

a doctoral student
who might have been our blood

donor sent us the worst
of it in camp-

fire lingo.

                    flummoxed,
we sexdanced

our way back
to the stegosaurus-
shaped truckstop:

it was high time

to start making
us some dioramas.

it was high time

to start getting recognized
for our woefully
cognitive goldmines.

how much more for the moonshine?

is not the question i want to hear when i've slumped into swanpose. or when i'm cradling an eyesore, outside, they are razoring off the necks of the other swans. it might look like a plan b, but it's not. yr crown is showing. so is his. lately, all we do is tell each other stories about things that happened to us before we met. last night, there were cherubim flinging flamefilled chandeliers at my head + everyone was making like dire panic. sometimes, i think to myself *what would* [redacted] *tell me to do if* [redacted] *+ I were still on speaking terms?* this me throwing water + crossing my arms, it's just a reflex. like that cat in the bathtub. o, if you could only learn to find my quirks endearing. tomorrow night, there's this party. i don't know if it's the kind of thing i'm supposed to dress up for or what.

we shall truth it ‘til it’s fake

too youth, i redress
ten times in
magnified morning

w/ poorly drawn
shades of hangover
helper. we are so far

out past country,
everything is water-
gun-colored.   yr ears

ring in roaches, but
i am still anxious
to knead into you,

pokeberry, to see
what else i can
pledge to the cause
of our self-defense.

o, the basic tenets of georgia belledome

adopted some beasts
to keep in a glass mouth
full of all kinds of milk.

especially unfortunate
is just who exactly

you think you are during
the low temperature

portion of the program.
traditionally, parting

gifts cause no small
amount of consternation

amongst the pear trees;
but this time around,

you are feeling uncomfortably
needed + ten hundred

thousand miles featherward,
things still won't spin
on their own accord.

after the second war of northern aggression

on yr blank days,
we take to picking

at that sad shard
of sheep you kept

in the giantess'
toenail before the last

occupation got
rather hyperterrain.

i sit on the front
porch w/ a tangle

of werewolf wiring—
you'd like to
take a nap,
but i know better.

you'd like to
whistle dixie

w/ yr teeth
trapped in uterine.

what to do w/ all these leftover easter eggs

call me–from the pulpit.
we went to church backwards.

there was a carpentry
+ an exposition in candles.

i never knew a baptism
from a toad horn.

let's clasp! let's lisp!
this thumbtack rolled

under trouble song is catching
up all the attention. lately, it's not that

difficult to be so diverting.   our arms
are sweaty under polyurethane lilies–some fat
drip for the greater good–betwixt the warding
off of promises + what might keep
                              + keep for another year yet.

delta darling

i hid the saw-
dust in the hearse

+ then picked
menial produce

whilst my fingers
bulged w/ broom

sore + insect
bite. the tornado

watch broke well
past full-druid.

i banjoed in
every space

that hadn't quite
tuned kismet.

i am betting on the horses,
you are betting on the hounds

opening day at the race tracks situated
behind the warzone, so everyone is under
the influence + queering

in polka dots— (take my bookie, please!)
such slattern, but it's still not as good
as the time i could be having in

my head. dollstain on the hotel
barstyle carpet—fetch me an ice bucket
+ my cellophane mask. (mala nostra,

everybody!) you are preening + droning
in the background (fizzy tizzy in a cup,
if you love her, look her up—).

some folk, they've come to consider this a minus—
me, i'm just happy that saxophonist
from memphis finally fell off the wagon again.

w/ ceremony: an afterparty

we passed the moated
place + let's admit

that i'm not that
amusing since the bell

fell off—i'll fetch a pink
core + a parasite

problem. but the urge
to lick at the back-

road tar keeps us rich
in inopportune moments.

            so, how is it that all of yr
other friends know

to attend to the units
of alligator conception

w/ out the taking off
of their formalwear?

            —they explain it so poorly,
say it probably

wasn't remotecontrolled—
but we were sure

you would find it
absolutely hilarious!

as if you circularsawed
through that sugarstump
                quite all by yrself.

the good copface

remonstrating
the vigil,
in plumlight
amongst the cropcircles
of what feels like florida, you initiate
something outlined
in bonechalk.

(like you now know help
is secret police
code *for do*
this for me, please.)

o, when the heart
starts up sore,
try not to humor
it. that screaming,
this cornsnake bite–
don't worry, it's only
there for show.

as you know.
now, put on those handcuffs

(baby,
make the good)
+ puckerup.

on the dangers of spending too much time w/ yr own kind

i heard you used to brighten
w/ vigilance, back before
you developed yr habit
of shaping onion
skins + stuft mice
into decorative ashtrays
+/or soapdishes. now, w/ a tin can meal grin,

you trash hump, w/ way less than a trial
or a tribulation. it may seem like you're in
transit, but you're not. this is yr wall made of packingpeanuts,
this is yr perpetual state of texas.
for you, i have all the timeouts in the world

while the sun gets on w/o
that soft orange twang
you're still o painfully pleased
to recognize.

when to form a prayer circle

back at the pancake house,
you try + convince us
that you are truly sorry
for the fire drill

+ all those misplaced
scissor kicks.
            the waitress in teal
            poly-everything

            wants to tell us about
            the 1, 2 sets
            of footprints she saw on
            the beach,

but you are still
so filled w/ something
quite terrible at living
a best life possible.

            baffled, she pulls a splinter
from yr tongue, a micro-
scope charm from yr legacy
bracelet.   o, honeydove!

we are all so fervent for you to finally
help you help yrself. we are all so fervent

for you to finally *feel* more like you
deserve to be up *there*,

            filled w/ hemoglobin
            + named by marquee-style lighting.

cakedirt

items will have shifted

my eardrums pop
whilst my solar
plexus aches
w/ emergency
situations.   i am chewing
tobacco + finding all
these dead pigeons
in yr travel-
sized dead pigeon
carrying case.
the flight attendant
squiggles at us.
but you are too busy
trying to make me feel
boring. eh, anyway,
we're both such prudes—
            something, something,
            something, *das kapital!*
look—here i am, my stiff
upper lip barely moistened
over these pilots accidentally
on the intercom,
debating whether or not
they should force
the wings to go counter-
clockwise or left-to-right.

radioactive housewifery

after work, you get cinema-mad
+ start novice waltzing

under the chandeliered sky.
we make a blackbeauty around

an atomically-correct bomb
shelter. i want to grow a clone w/ side-

burns on it before the century smashes
to or fro. this headache is warning me

that you've never been less hepcat.
still, we are all johnnygirl: pre-genius,

post-warhero + i am wanting to clean
the entire surface area of this time

capsule devoted to our neato! domesticbliss.

the trouble w/ empty containers

before going to bed, you spray all yr friends w/ glue made out of hooves + horns. they die quick but painful deaths. you spend the night dreaming that you're snorkeling in the gulf of mexico + meremaids are giving you high-fives w/ the bottoms of their mermaid tails.

you wake up to find that every previously empty container in your apartment is now sprouting a new friend: teacups, bags from the grocery store, the mopwater bucket, that plastic lining of what used to be a vanillacherry-scented candle, pill bottles leftover from last year's breastbone surgery, some of late aunt susan's striped + polka-dotted hatboxes, yr bellybutton (the first time in yr life you wish you were an outie...), a doll carriage, a cracked piggybank + a purple suede purse yr dad sent you on yr brother's birthday (b/c, lately, he's had a really hard time keeping up w/ things like who was born when).

most of the new friend heads have mouths, the mouths whine that they are thirsty from the toes on up. you can't see any toes. or even arms. the new friends w/ mouths claim their toes are welded to the bottoms of the previously empty containers.

you spray these new friends w/ what's left of the glue made out of hooves + horns, but you don't really have enough to do any damage. now the new friends are angry b/c they get that you're trying to send them into an untimely but quick but painful grave. the new friends start listing all the problems w/ yr body + yr home décor.

you feel the beginnings of a panic attack coming on. you curl up in the cabinet under the kitchen sink + call up yr stepmom, who is a psychic + a dentist (though these talents never get used simultaneously). yr stepmom says not to worry, that something similar happened to her back when she was in her mid-twenties, before she married yr dad. yr stepmom tells you to get out of the cabinet + pack up like you're getting ready to run errands. she tells you to remain calm, to make steady eye contact w/ the new friends, but to refrain from speaking. she says to stop listening to them, as if you can help it. once you get out of the building, she says, get on the anonymous FBI tipline + tell them that there are terrorists residing at yr address.

this sounds like a reasonable plan, except for one small detail. you ask yr stepmom but what about the new friend growing in yr bellybutton. yr stepmom, who's an outie, sighs + tells you that there are some problems best discussed between you + yr real mother. so you call up yr real mother, but she just gives you the same advice about making calm eye contact + tipping off the FBI.

try not to fuss too much over the way i dot my *i's*

no one can read my cursive script—
i wanted to lap in the dolphin tank

but it was the last   + worst
day of our period piece.   let's lace

w/ black sea laudanum.   our post-rash
everything bumped in the dark.

                              there is some possibility
that i'll never really feel fluently in anything—

                                          a physical cowardice
                    vs.   a mental cowardice.

but, hey, thank christ they rarely go together!
xxxxxx   xxxxxxxxx   xxxxxxxxxxxxxxxxx.

hear those trumpets under the much-maligned.
this is maybe offensive, but i am working

                    on coming off as less immigrant,
like if it's really spring, then my neck flops sideways

+ then everyone knows i'm in heinous need
                              of another resort-style vacation.

w/ you, every night is '80s night

+ the morning after,
we are out of coffee,
but still sporting
the occasional nice
+ lilac-like feature.
a mixed tape of that whale
who can only sing at 51.75 Hz
is causing me to go
practically goth.
here is some eyeliner
along w/ more pet
rocks for you to name.
o, please stop
asking if i am fairy
or faux-ovaried—
i don't want us to
to start getting all
socioeconomical at a time
that could be as good as this.

she's eating dirt like it's cake
(+ really terrible at flirting)

many miracles have
happened, but
they didn't fix up
much of anything.
like most female geese
w/ a digestive system
still located on the left
side of the abdomen,
she reckoned to get on
some of that micromath
medicine, though it was already
too little +/or too late.
honky had spoil liver,
swole feet; a rough
approximation of
cookbook, pg. 6. all month,
we've been girl-
sad for her + her pushed-
out terrorhole lined
in leftover golddust.

all in favor say *neigh*

you are a two
+/or three-
trick pony living
clopped down
past the tracks
w/ jingle belly
+ a belief in everything
tasting like saltlicked.
so, let's reign it in,
glittersaddle: i can
tell you about my ranch-
hand, but i can't
give you a straight answer
as to whether or not
you are merely being
settled for
                    +/or on. i mean, let's
not put this in horsemouth,
i don't think we are forever
yet, don't go waiting for me
to start unslinging my insides
any time even close to soon.

there are two passwords: they do not rhyme, but they both begin w/ the letter 'c'

the insurgency offers you a fulcrum + some viruses w/ exceptionally clever codenames. under the paraffin lamp, yr contact's expression is perfect for ham radio hour. you both lisp dreadfully: he has a set of dead locusts sewn to the cuffs of his gloves + you two are growing into that strained kind of intimacy that gets real political, real quick. tell him that every other night there is to be a tactical error on the part of the rape prevention unit. that once you repeat a thing three times, it becomes twice as funny. you don't know whether or not he is really in on the cache situated behind the orphanage project, but both of you are next in line for some blue + green ribbons, *if* you can manage to stay away from getting o so nervous. this is especially difficult during the rainy season. you know, he says, whenever something pulls in yr chest, just throw tomatoes at it. or, sometimes, it can help to imagine that the other parties are in their underwear, drinking water that tastes kind of funny to them too.

when keeping the upperhand is everything

they shyed out
all nite on
the dent in

the chartreuse
cushion, quite
pretending to listen

+ not notice
each other's south-
mouths. freshly

scabbed, it was time
to get significantly
more or less

drunk. someone
somewhere else
was going to have

to spend the rest
of his or her life
circling around

that west park statue
dedicated to the giving
            of bad news first.

a complicated relationship w/ all the other women in yr life

yr sister killed those gerbils
b/c there wasn't enough

to do in the upper
peninsula anyway.

even if we're both traveling
incognito, it is still daylight

savings time + i am still
moving yr mother to tears (j/k!).

one of the aunties, she pinned this lingerie
to the insides of my trenchcoat.

we need to start preparing
for the next government

raid. especially if we're really going
to inherit yr grandmother's make-
                    yr-own-militia problem.

it was a good day to be a second runner up

we were in a petite
frame pageant, so nothing more

got expected save posing thru the sash-
tying ceremony held under

veins hoistedhigh by the shortcircuiting host.

can't believe you got points off
for yr answer about the genetic
manipulation of lab rats.

so, sparkling like tiaras, we get back to the $150
hotel + watch kung-fu movies
in high def till i'm puking cornsyrup in snowflake
shapes. a rap at the door + after 30 seconds,
it left. most folk, they like
pretty things, but pretty people make them

morethan a littlebit nervous.

better the devil you don't

ugh, the triple-sixed beast
we know is so wrung-

out, is so stuck behind furniture
too heavy to move w/o help

from our creepy-ass neighbors.

the only thing left in our brag-
bag is an uncanny ability

to hold our tongues + remain
perfectly expressionless.

we never even *attempt* the above-
bed dartboard.   don't feel

noah-level thunderstorm, feel
barely there weather under

itchy-cheap hat. i mean, *help*.
i mean, i'm trapped inside

the great american red-horned
*whal*e named after yr mother

+ i would like to get home
again some time before dark.

fairytale in which i am an irresponsible pet-sitter

there are so many beds i could pass out in, but they are all fairly uncomfortable +/or too recently occupied. every three days, i change the sheets of my own bed b/c stray colors keep curling up under the pillows + dyeing themselves to death.

i am never having children. if i was less selfish, i would have mentioned this before my teeth started chipping the teacups. everyone says i can't do anything right, that i am so sad, like a unicorn covered in scabies. this probably isn't a surprise, but i'm never going to be thin again. most of my extra-germanic orifices are filled w/ troll paste + dead gingerbread dough.

yesterday morning, i disguised myself as a stepsister + wandered around the forest asking for opinions about myself. one of the talking trees said that i seemed to be doing well, that i still looked like a natural brunette. the tree said he had heard i was careless w/ other smaller living creatures though, that nobody in the forest really believed there was nothing i could have done to prevent the wizard's parakeet from drowning in less than two inches of water.

like, i already know everything there is to know about our government's involvement in alien abductions

it turns out all
these spaceclouds

+ all these silos
shaped like spaceclouds

are part of a superterranean
plan to spread

eagle you in a cornfield
like an inalienable right,

like everyone at the roller
rink was only pretending

to forget yr birthday,
like, i didn't even know

i was white trash,
like, how many grams of muscle

to move an ounce of bone?
                                        like, ask me
anything: my hands are sweaty

w/ mid-july, this room
is getting shiny mid-ways

thru a night that just
got really fucking weird.

we've always been a little bit space cadet

hey houston!
set the tripwire,
salt my space slug-
heart. yr phone
number starts
w/ 555 when
i sire up
a slice of smile
+ hold or fold
yr truth or dare cards.
let's springspring
on the up + up.
b/c all of us deserve
better than a yes or less.
let's use therapyspeak
to torture the rest
of the crew.
let's get everyone to believe
that earthquakes
on mars
aren't even
called earth-
quakes anymore.

double dutch duchess

for the past pale month,
i've been wearing this
burlap sash under
a really wrong
impression as to
what constitutes
a *professional* trans-
siberian-superstar
+ who knows what
time it is—
            my managers keep telling
            us that they certainly don't
+ the tabloids should start
alleging that i've got
this bad case of crushcatchers.

because, lately, i am feeling all

            threshing floor-like—
there are gemstone-sized
bugs everywhere you look.
            o, so, pinch me. o, so,

            therefore, my dear adoring
public, please be informed
that, from here on out,
i can no longer abide
by being addressed
by my stage name
or confirmation number.

we are running out of quality;
we are running out of quantity

there's a stable full of red sea-
horses tethered to my side

of the bed + this furniture
is starting to look

like it belongs to a school
of dentistry.

i'm trying

to get them to leave me,
siren-made + in the corner.

i'm not feeling
up for another hour of smelling

salt therapies. o, i know,
that when you realize

i have something growing
on my opera-knowing bones,

you will clarify, you will start
getting used to making

do w/ our third
+ fourth best options.

things to do in personform
(when nothing is better than something)

to interfaith. to ghosttour. :::: to chainsaw. to translate.

to stop quittingsmoking w/ experts. :::: to slanderfox.

to clamour jukebox, jukecircle. :::: to dummydumdum.

to friendofthefamily. :::: to torque w/nighthanger.

tocovet. to covet. :::: to tourist in shortsight.

to peer out like unfresh plucked. :::: to drilldown. o deepsinking.

to ready, to heavy in the eyesore. :::: to drink the memory out of.

to unrally the whistles + balloons. :::: to evoke in morguedark.

@the loudest waiting room ever in the history of the world

the taffeta was on
insideout + my self-
esteem is so lowbrow.

we're all easily aroused
by broken glass sea-
gulls in dead bottles.

some fixing to hearken
back to the instrumental,
nevermind the woodland

creatures +/or animalzzzz.
or, if under great duress—
take my pulse to prove

you're virgin + yonder-
shape again, that we're just
here to further conflate

healthiness w/ happiness,
honeystick w/ such a thing
as being too fashionably late.

winter dosages for the emotionally challenged

she picked a place
past the steeples
+ handles messy
quite well now.
even after the iceberg
pulled itself through
+ through
the eyeneedle,
we took to stepsistering.
a man in
her bed is dangerous
+ a woman
in her bed
is embarrassing. somebody
keeps fucking
with the radiator.
i wanted to
make a fist
for her to shake
like a cold-
brained albatross.
lantern-lit,
we agreed to maintain
the pioneers'
museum at cost.
            the helicopter
            ride cured us
            of our hiccups.
it's fine, we both have
really good insurance. nobody
has to sculpt a snowflora
for the person they came with–
but, still, i'm staying on
whatever point
of the spectrum
she's staying on.

garden partying for geniuses

all lounge in flora
formations w/ soft edges
tucked in dripping togas,
they refuse + rejoice asymmetrically.
          but [the real 'we'] consistently
keeps trace amounts of secret
[from the real 'them'].

[the real 'we'] levitate over the burning trees.
[the real 'we'] undress the clouds.
[the real 'we'] levitate over the burning trees
                    while serenading the stratosphere.
          —these are the perfect circumstances
          for keeping one onethousandth
          of the fauna exotic in our arms—

a nothing separated outside [the real 'we'].
the ground got small + stoneage,
it fell further + further past sea level.

[the real 'we'] + the rest decided to quit exhaling
               as if we weren't already born yesterday.

the wardens' biannual gala

nobody knows what day it is; but it is probably saturday or sunday. the warden's children are maxing the foyer w/ the wardens' favorite colors. you are rehearsing yr *thankyou* or *sorry* danse.

the wardens require extra attention as many of their children have already collapsed unto themselves. you suspect that there are several different versions of the seating chart—since the redistribution of time zones, rsvps seem rather beside the point.

one of the wardens' children ties a smileface to the handle of a pair of minute-cutting scissors. another of the wardens' children paints sundials on the floor.

the other employees arrive w/ vintage meters sewn onto the tops of their dansing slippers. except for the one employee who arrives inside an enormous strawberry cake—he isn't wearing slippers at all. the wardens' children + you entertain the room by making choo-choo sounds w/ nicely-inlaid harelips.

someone comes in + asks to see the wardens' childrens' papers. the someone goes away when the wardens presents her w/ a crack-free pocket watch of western descent.

the wardens give the signal—the wardens' children + you start discretely waving camphor rags under the other employees' noses. the lights in the control room flicker but don't go off. one of the wardens remarks that it's pretty much as if the clock had it in for them.

dirge for a creature of consequence

yr blood pumped off
like a very sick sloth,
but you are finally
thinking to +/or for
yrself.   you've always smelled
so good, like you grew up in a house
w/ a backyard + that backyard
was full of cherry nose + bee bombs.

.

.

but surely you still have some estranged emotions
ready to haunt about my parts?   .

.

.

now, no one can even handshake.
someone calls you exotic—
this is supposed to be a compliment,
but, of course, it's not.

.

.

but surely you still have some estranged emotions
ready to haunt about my parts?

.

.

now we ground up an anchor
+ sprinkle it over yr cleansheet
until you sink to the bottom
of the charming, charming dirthole.

whereas we indulge in the recreational use of circular logistics

in full view of the sometimes red hospital,
we round our hands around the body

of a tough-luck bird. we are appareled
in makes + models we're both already

too old for. the circumference of my witch-
burnt finger is swelling, is maybe saving some

lives after sundown. let's watch the planets turn
catherine wheels while we plan our next

great american shortcut. i mean, let's just go ahead
+ infer mars-chimes, subtract my negative

thoughts from yrs until we can revel in the plain
fact that, even though neither of us is getting any

happier, at least one of us is getting less + less sad.

the best kind of climate control

underneath yr feet,
the elements warp

into masonform. i hold
my breath + yrs. let's dangle
a token zero in front

of yr winning birthday
+/or lottery ticket, let's look into
the more avian side of the sky.

                    sans cancer,
we can taxidermy the sun.
i want what you want unless want
is more than mere intemperance
                    mixed w/ fire strips.

it's not what you think, but how you think it

it's not what you think

o, let me ease
into my terribletricks.

take me to the drop of land
filled w/ neardeath trees.

you can be winner
'til the skies retract,
i can be pearl,
            a pushed apex wrapped
            in paralyzing white.

this is our wholeworld now,
pixilated w/ reptiles who don't
have enough skin to form a proper eyelid.

but how you think it

no, stop me from diseasing
out of my wonderfultreats.

leave me in the middle of the ocean
emptied of far-away-from-life rocks.

you can't be a loser
before the ground expands,
i can't be a pearl
            a pulled nadir unwrapped
            in the free-floating black.

this isn't our halfworld then,
all of the reptiles have more than enough
skin to form a proper eyelid.

Acknowledgments

"(the south is only a home)" is the title of a song by The Fiery Furnaces.

Earlier versions of this manuscript have previously appeared in the chapbook *halfsteps + cloudfang* (plumberries press). Earlier versions of this manuscript have appeared in the following journals: *Alice Blue, Barn Owl Review, Barrelhouse, Bone Bouquet, Concert at Chopin's Opera House II, Drupe Fruits, Everyday Genius,* Featherproof Books' *Storigami Project, GlitterPony, Humble Humdrum Cotton Frock, Jubilat, Night Train, PANK Magazine, PANK Magazine's 2011 Queer Issue, Sixth Finch,* Small Fire Press' *Matchbook Vol. 3, We Are So Happy To Know Something,* and *Zero Ducats.*

Daniela Olszewska

Daniela Olszewska is the author of two other forthcoming collections of poetry: *Citizen J* (Artifice Books) and *How To Feel Confident With Your Special Talents* (co-written with Carol Guess) (Black Lawrence Press). She sits on Switchback Books' Board of Directors and teaches creative writing in conjunction with The Alabama Prison Arts & Education Project.